Connie Valentine 11/09
2001

Lives of Others

Patricia Fargnoli

OYSTER RIVER

Copyright © 2001 by Patricia Fargnoli

ISBN 1-882291-61-1

Printed in Canada

Acknowledgments

Chile Verde Review: Arguing Life for Life, Fate
The Comstock Review: Diana, For a Blind Friend
Connecticut River Review: The Swankeeper, Diamond in Concert, The People Upstairs, The Cameo Carvers of Torre Del Greco
Connecticut Writer: The Undertaker's Wife
Crab Orchard Review: For a Composer at Eighty-three
Flyway: Hardscrabble in Marlow, New Hampshire
Granite Review: Guide at the Norman Rockwell Museum
Green Mountains Review: Vathanna Tells of Her Hunger
Indiana Review: Gas Station Santa
Poetry Northwest: The Phenomenology of Garbage, Locked
Poet's On: Donor
Yankee: Low Tide, Blues, Pemaquid Sunset

Boundaries, Hopper's Paintings, Dublin Beggar, first appeared in *Necessary Light* Utah State University Press, Logan, UT 1999

Cover is a detail from "Rooms for Tourists," a painting by Edward Hopper, 1945, at the Yale University Art Museum.

OYSTER RIVER PRESS
20 RIVERVIEW ROAD · DURHAM, NEW HAMPSHIRE 03824 · 603-868-5006

*They were lost and unacquainted —
till they found themselves in* OTHERS,
*Who had groped as they were groping
where dim ways were perilous.*

– Edwin Arlington Robinson, "The Three Taverns"

I bid him look into the LIVES *of men as though into a mirror* . . .

– Terence (195 OR 185–159 B.C.), *Adelphoe.*

Those who write about life, reflect about life . . .
you see in OTHERS *who you are.*

– Bernard Malamud, *Dublin's Lives*

CONTENTS

Lives of Others 3
Boundaries 4
Hopper's Paintings 6
Diana 7
For a Blind Friend 8
Spring Song for Robin 9
Poem for a Composer at Eighty-Three 10
The Swankeeper 12
Low Tide, Blues, Pemaquid Sunset 13
Diamond in Concert 14
Gas Station Santa 15
Hardscrabble in Marlow, New Hampshire 17
The Roadside Spring at Yale Forest 18
Guide at The Norman Rockwell Museum 20
The Phenomenology of Garbage 22
The People Upstairs 24
Undertaker's Wife 25
Fate 26
Locked 28
Donor 30
Dublin Beggar 32
Vathana Tells of Her Hunger 34
The Cameo Carvers of Torre Del Greco 37
Arguing Life for Life 39

Lives of Others

LIVES OF OTHERS

They brush up against me
walking so close their shadows
cover me before they slide by
and disappear, the way deer
on the island leave the field
when I surprise them,
though they can't go far.
Between us, an old light
shimmers like mountain-peak ice
seen at a distance.
How important they are to me,
the other lives, vital as air,
lustrous and full of histories,
each one beginning and ending alone
but spreading colors into the earth
that holds our footsteps in patterns —
an interlace of closeness and distance,
as if we were cells in the same body,
our blood running the same vessels.
Isn't it odd how sometimes
the most ordinary face coming toward me
down a street loud with people
seems beautiful, how often there's a shine
of recognition, the slightest smile for instance,
or eyes that suddenly fasten on mine?
In those few seconds
I am bound to that stranger.

BOUNDARIES

All week I will be driving to the seminar
in Concord; all week I will be passing
a red-bearded construction worker
by the side of Route 9 in the 7 a.m. sun.
Light flares off the gold hair on his forearms;

red dust rises all around him.
They are building a new road
and he holds a wooden pointer at the boundary
between the shoulder and the one passable lane.
He keeps cars going like cows through a chute.

He wears a yellow hard hat,
doesn't look up,
and the next day he sits in the same position,
the same folding chair.
I begin to imagine he's been there all along

holding the pointer through the wide afternoon
letting dusk settle around his shoulders,
keeping it steady all night.
I wonder what he thinks about all day
in the clouds of exhaust, in the heat rising.

The following day, for miles past him
I construct him a life: a trailer,
wife bringing corn bread and beans to him,
a beer, maybe two, television to light
their evening, the bed moving under them.

At night in my dream he appears at my door
holding a bouquet of Joe-Pye-Weed,
asking me to change his life.
Day in, day out, all that week I think about him —
while I'm walking the dog, weeding tomatoes.

He is the fixed point;
I am nothing to him
in the endless line of bumpers passing.
Today, certain I'm invisible,
I drive past a last time. He is standing

watching the bulldozer roll the earth over
but suddenly he turns — and against the blur
of dust lifting and sun falling
in rivers of light through the trees,
he looks up — he waves at me.

I keep the intimacy of that instant,
past mile markers, past the low marsh,
past the dark grove of white pine,
and milkweed releasing froth to the wind —
past the wood ducks that fly parallel to my car window,

then dive down toward the lucent black eye of a pond.

HOPPER'S PAINTINGS

The ones I like best are the ones with windows lit up:
"Rooms for Tourists," "House at Dusk."
In those there is a cool inner glow at least —
and with it hope of warmth, however insubstantial,
against the shadows of the night
which fall down over everything.
I can imagine the people inside of them,
solitary yes, and yet not utterly lonely,
perhaps reading or passing slowly from room to room,
a hairbrush or toothpaste in their hand.
And the phone a silent instrument on the hall table —
a kind of peace emanating from the receiver
and from the lightbulbs overhead
which are overloaded with silence.
The compartments of the houses are as enclosed
as the berths on an old Pullman
where, as a child, I rocked and rocked to the round
metal repetitions of the wheels,
not terribly concerned about where I was going,
the tunnel ahead, the rusted bridge we might pass over,
or the torn cities beyond it.

DIANA

When she walks she is like those pictures
of Shiva, her arms, hips, legs moving
at unpredictable angles.
And she lives in danger of falling —
so I am always reaching, not quite touching her,
my hands ready beneath her jutting elbows.

When she tries to speak her mouth stretches wide,
phlegm gargling in her throat, what words she has left
willing themselves into form through the tongue
that turns back on her missing teeth.

Swallow Diana, I say, *Speak slowly. Swallow.*
What she wants to say is what she loves:
flower, water, kiss, the names of her daughters
and the roll call of her dead — all to Huntington's,
handed down: two grandmothers, aunt, mother.

Trying to understand, I ask her to name
the month and the town. These are April's last days
when leaves are not leaves but frail yellow flowers.
As if trying to gather clues, she rolls her eyes
toward the glass, toward the hills that surround us.
Spring? she asks in a whisper, *I think it's Spring?*

Beyond the window, forsythias trail necklaces
as twisted as strands of DNA —
and everything that can, begins again.

FOR A BLIND FRIEND

Wanting to understand a universe
where maps are nothing but counting and sound,
where *making love* means *quilts* and *satin*
and words like *blue* are only a statement
for what's never been known,
I've dreamed my way into blindness
as a kind of sad game, tying a band
of white muslin over my eyes, going out
the way someone might go into rain —
eyes closed, face turned up like a dish to the weather.

Your dreams are all memories of voices, of touch:
your mother's *Damn you* as shrill now in your mind
as before her death, the beer-slurred
Get outta my way of your father, his slap
across her face so clear that you took each
whole argument in, stored inflections,
all the violent words. Escape impossible,
you huddle still in your childhood
and thirty years later you chant those words to me
as though you might wring from them
some bitterroot essence of love.

Late afternoon sun floods my double window
and you give me your hand, your voice —
but you exist in a landscape I cannot imagine,
measuring distance from buildings by the echo
of your stick on the walk, naming friends
by the weight of their footfall.
Oh Carla, there is a vast river between us
I cannot cross — a black and turbulent water.

SPRING SONG FOR ROBIN

A woodthrush sings in Robin's woods.
I haven't heard it, though I will.
She hears its music in the evenings,
from her two-room home backed into a hill.

I haven't heard it, though I will,
where Monadnock rises like a hat
near her pine-board home backed into a hill
where Robin lives with her querulous cat.

Where Monadnock rises like a hat
beyond the simple cabin door
where Robin lives with her querulous cat,
where Robin sweeps her kitchen floor.

Beyond the open cabin door
she hears its voice ring through the evening.
While Robin sweeps the kitchen floor,
a woodthrush sings in Robin's woods

near her two-room home backed into the hill.
I haven't heard it, though I will.

POEM FOR A COMPOSER AT EIGHTY-THREE

for Juli Nunlist

So we go into the old
        House where Juli lives
To hear her compositions

Of Rilke's poems, a cycle:
        Du gehst mit, Lied vom Meer,

You come too, Song from the sea,
        And the others, sung
On tape by the soprano

Who gets them exactly right —
        Each note expressing grief, and

Longing, along with beauty —
        Without which, the best
Music, like the world, would be

Nothing. So silent we keep —
        In the small, beamed, wainscotted

Room with its watercolor
        Of Versailles' gardens,
The blue Chinese hand-hooked rug —

Following the hand-inked score,
        Listening hard with our hearts.

The music expands the room —
        Juli bends toward us
The frail stem of her mortal

Body. She watches our faces,
    Her own face, unlined, shining

And beatific, as if
    Already she has
Been in the heavenly world.

THE SWANKEEPER

In his weathered punt he paddles out —
old man pulling back water,
the clouded Thames water. He knows
this current, its swirls and backflows,
how the tide tugs at Traitor's Gate,
climbs Wapping House stairs,
how the sea calls it home.

All day his mind is filled with swans,
the Queen's swans, their plumes
billowing beneath Tower Bridge,
arcs and curves on black water.
For them he dips oars into each new day,
letting mist into his bones.

How he loves to herd and mark them,
trapping their fullness between bent arm and rib
as if those royal heartbeats could liven his own.
Around him river music rises,
winch-groan and clang of shipyards,
gulls yawk and clatter.

When sunset draws him back again
to the solid shore, he takes this music
home with him to fill his sleep
as the swans fill his sleep, their wings
a flurry through the long night —
as though anyone could keep them.

LOW TIDE, BLUES, PEMAQUID SUNSET

The last beached fish still flips, the fisherman hauls
his bent bow in again, young wife behind him on the sand,
sleeping son held to her shoulder. Gulls' steep calls
ride the wide waves, orange wash narrows to a coral band.

The man, how young he is — each honed limb burned
to tarnished bronze. Woman and child trapped in shadow.
How fathomless the small one's sleep, how silently
the woman stands — like the star of the sea.

How many hours will she wait — the man hefting one last blue
he stows with his stack on the sand? She shifts the child, pulls
him back from dream. Darkness rides in and paws
the ground. Patient as she, the gulls line the seawalls.

DIAMOND IN CONCERT

He is all center, all sun as he plays
to us, song after song, his voice reaching
out to our sixteen thousand bodies,
a few of us already standing, some
swaying, our faces open and wanting,
his words washing over the dullness,
convincing us that in this vast temple
someone at last understands.
We reach out, all of us —
front row gyrators, the grandmother
whose son bought tickets for Christmas, the guy
in the hockey shirt, all of us clapping
until blood pounds in our palms,
as the music crescendos
and the house lights go on
and off, and we are all together,
all standing and there is no stopping
between songs, they are coming quickly
as the breaths of someone making love:
all the old ones, the ones we sing loudly,
and he goads us on, the lights flickering
purple to lime-green — dizzy with yellow.
He never stops singing, spinning, dipping,
never stops punching the air,
all that applause
flooding over him until his face is
a map of sweat and ecstasy and we
have tears in our eyes as we call out
in one voice, in one breath
as if this music
was all we needed —
all we could ever desire.

GAS STATION SANTA

You lift my day, cherry-cheeked hustler
pumping gas in your oil-grimy red velvet suit
and your square glassless glasses.
You scurry, old and bent, from car to car,
like some befuddled gone-seedy saint,
squeegeeing windows, leaning in to ask:
what and how much?
Your white ermine's worn to shabby gray
and your gas-stained trousers bag

over your flat-bottomed bottom beneath
the wide black belt your belly bulges over.
I'll even forgive you for giving me that blank stare
when I tell you I think you're going
to show up in a poem.
Bottom line — I can see you're not much
to pin my hopes on, and I'd be hard put
to raise you to the power

of the magical old North Pole story
but I can tell by the pole star glint
in your eye when you say: *Nine dollars even,*
that you mean well enough
and your milky beard curls
like a silky thing I might want
to run through my fingers. You're all
I've got after all,
so I'll make up my mind to believe in you,

and when you take my last twenty
with a not-too-much-in-a-rush smile
and bring back a wad of ones saying

Here you are — as if I hadn't known
where I was all along —
(Sunoco, West Street,
two days before Christmas),
I'll stuff the bills back in my wallet
without even bothering to count them.

HARDSCRABBLE IN MARLOW, NEW HAMPSHIRE

The builder must have taken a bunch of boards
and nailed them, helter-skelter up,
one room of the house strung to another,
not quite straight
but jutting out in bent nonsensical angles,
kitchen nailed to bedroom, porch off the bath,
tilted apartment staggering off back,
and then the shed — where no one even meant to keep
boards straight or close, the sky falls through.
Once built, the house spent its life falling down,
red clapboards faded to dried-blood brown,
pitted by sleet and the years unpainted,
chicken coop sway-backed and weathered gray,
sweet peas trailing neglect in the garden,
chickens scruffy, grass grown to bull thistle
and thorn, screens torn, three trucks
rusting roadside — business the owner has given up.
Where life is unhooked as a one-hinged screen door —
a tipsy barn half-stands, half-falls
against the three-blue-surround
of staggered hills and an algae-green pond.
A hard man tractors an obstinate field
and a woman whose eyes look numb as snow,
shucks a bucket of peas on a wooden-slat chair.

THE ROADSIDE SPRING AT YALE FOREST

A guy in Levis and a Nashville sweatshirt
gets out of a sedan with a black trash bag
of bottles and sits on the low granite ledge,
holding a milk bottle to the spigot.
Then an elderly woman
drives up and gets out.
She's pure New Hampshire and has
"Live free or die" written all over her face.
I get out too so she won't get ahead of me.
But she only wants to stand in the shadow
of those sweet-smelling white pines.

And she wants to talk — so we all say good morning
and the man points out the warning posted on the fence —
that reminds me about the Sentinel article —
how the bank has foreclosed
on the farm around the bend
and the spring is in danger
because developers want to build ten movie theaters,
a supermarket and a Home Depot.

And we all think something should be done
because the spring has been here longer
than any of us can remember. Forever, really.
And everyone comes here because of Keene water
which smells like eggs and sometimes runs red.

The spring's been here, I say, since I came up
from Connecticut to escape the interstate.
It's been here, (she says) since she finished
nurse's training at Boston Children's.
It's been here, he says, since his childhood at least.

It was here when he went to Nam and when
he left again for an insurance career in Massachusetts —
it was here when he came back.

The article said there have been town meetings
where the people stood up and said: No. Or Yes.
And meetings where only the town council was allowed to talk —
the talk: about wetlands, zoning, taxes, progress.
And there have been letters to the editors —
Yes. And No.
And because all *that* has been done and what more
can anyone do anyway,
we all stand around, three strangers,
and shake our heads as our bottles fill up with water.

GUIDE AT THE NORMAN ROCKWELL MUSEUM

This time of year no entrance fee to pay.
The winter months we don't get many folk —
anyway no heater in the back.
Out there's so cold that we don't run
the picture show. Bound to freeze up if we did.
Let me show you a few of these I'm in:
that one from the Boyscout calendar "The Rescue."
Nineteen-thirty-eight, New England Flood.
I was four, so pretty, yellow curls 'n all.
The water up within an inch of the bridge,
me wrapped in patchwork in the Boyscout's arms.

You can't buy one, all the prints are sold —
been sold for years; thank you for asking though.
We used to have a figurine of it.
Guess things go — one way or another —
something always coming to take their place.
This one's my favorite — "Christmas Homecoming."
It made the cover of Saturday Evening Post.
That was Jason, his eldest, coming home,
his mother, Mary Rockwell, hugging him —
that's me on the right, about thirteen I was,
and Norman, standing proud as punch with his children.

Both dead now. How long? I lose track. Time goes
by fast as the neighbor boy on his bike
and don't come back. I'm fifty-five this year
and not ashamed to be, or to tell it to you.
Did I say this used to be a church?
Those scenes of Christ's life on the ceiling —
some unknown painter done 'em around

nineteen hundred — a Frenchman wandering through.
Lots more out back. You'll find "The Four Freedoms"
up where the altar used to be. What's it like
to be immortalized, you say? Don't know —
too busy living through these days I guess.

THE PHENOMENOLOGY OF GARBAGE

She is sitting there watching the garbage man
who pulled in as she was about to back out,
his green and white truck
blocking her way, so there's nothing to do
but watch as he climbs down from the cab
and goes around to the barn to haul out barrels.
Because every moment's
an occasion for attention,
she notices the name *Cheshire Sanitation,*
and it makes her wonder what's being sanitized,
certainly not yesterday's turkey
along with the Boston Globe,
and a popped volley ball,
cranked down into the dark dragon maw
and smashed into some essence
of turkey/ball/Globe,
that makes her think of Zen,
how everything's connected.
And not the truck which smells like rotten pears;
and not the barrels, filthy, but emptied out
for now of what she doesn't want —
the unendable excess.
And because she can't go anywhere,
she sits there (in her old Toyota Corolla
with the rusty gash on its side)
as the grind
of the compactor drowns out
her dog singing in the barn, nose in the air,
and she wonders where all this stuff is going —
(not to the dump, which is obvious)

but in the long run —
matter, not able to be created or destroyed —
the atoms of some long-gone Magna Charta
perhaps even now storming around in her blood,
kicking up her irritable bowel,
or hurtling this precise minute
(in the leftover turkey leg bone)
down into the compactor —
Being brought forward
all the way from the Big Bang,
the whole mess collapsing
to no-time and all-time
the way everything's a paradox,
like her thoughts which seem to be going
everywhere and nowhere . . .
which are at a dead end
and no end (so to speak), blocked
by this metal Magog rumbling before her.

THE PEOPLE UPSTAIRS

You would think that in bed at least
I'd be safe. When they come in
from the second shift at the post office,
my ceiling shakes. The nights he beats her
there are thuds and hour on hour of walking.
There is the wounded cheetah of her voice.
Beneath them, I lie alone in the long darkness,
imagining myself wounded under the snow
and unable to speak of it.

The night I called the police
they had been knocking each other around
the floor for hours, their tumult
breaking through the whirr of my fan.
When the cops took him away
the stillness was strange, almost unbearable.

But tonight she takes him back —
feet climbing stairs, the old patterns of steps
above me, and I wonder at how easily she forgives.

UNDERTAKER'S WIFE

Nightly your hands smooth my stomach, my sides,
all the small pulses beneath my skin.

Your hands, soft as the gray pockets
I slip my silver in, and I try to forget

how all day they've been searching the flesh
of anonymous bodies, rouging cheeks, arranging spirals

of hair — as if death could be made beautiful, the way
as a young girl I loitered with Ultima and Coral Bloom

for hours before the steamy glass,
preparing for the first love of my life.

From you I've learned how close to death love is:
insensible rush of emotion, the sudden awareness

that no one will ever again speak
with the exact accent of this one,

that no one could copy the particular
shrug of these shoulders.

And loss, whether from death or love,
comes to mean some part of myself flown off.

Now, for example, you,
stripped of your formal black suit,

are like a white and luminous bird, your wings
folding and unfolding above me,

the shape of your feathers like exclamations
against the blackness of this bedroom.

FATE

Before the crash itself,
the impact of metal on wood,
the house collapsing,
a whirl of wind shoved her ten feet back
from the exact spot in her kitchen where
(in the next moment)
the car rammed through, leaving its proof:
skid marks on the gleaming floor.
Dazed, she stood clenching
her husband's trousers, his empty form,
the lint of their lives
coming off in her hands.

Sun glared in the opening.

How to make sense of it?
In the backyard, the cows and the goat
bent their dumb mouths to devour
her well-tended grass for no reason
beyond hunger and the next moment's need.
She was surprised by her own mouth
which was screaming as she ran
her hands over her body
in the kitchen of poppy curtains.

Not a scratch on her, not an ort of dirt,

only the cold glaze of whole skin.
As when ice snakes
a mere black skim on the pond,
the pond where the red Beretta

had come to an upended stall, where inside it,
the woman —
the one she might have been —
sat stuporous and smiling
in the driver's seat.

LOCKED

Back from a flat-out day in New York, the museum,
the bus squeals into Hartford, drops us on a badly lit
dead-end at ten p.m., one block from the ghetto.

Some idiot has locked our cars behind the ten-foot
wrought iron fence and padlocked chain-linked gates.
We bang on the chains; no guard anywhere.

We call police; they don't come. We flag down
a firetruck. They say they've no right to break in
and don't do a damn thing for us.

Exhausted, thirsty, we lean against the fence
in the blue city dark. From a tenement's second story,
a woman belts out an aria of pain:

Fuck you, you liar, you fucking asshole.
Above the cries of a child, above the raped-woman
howl of a siren, she belts it.

I know you're cheating. I can't take it.
I'm leaving.
Do you hear me? I'm leaving now.

We might be sitting in a theater where the picture's
gone dark, that's how bigger-than-life, almost mythic,
her voice is, pouring through the clouded night,

across backyards, across the universe.
She might be singing for all of us, so cold, so numb
in our own dead-end, wanting water, wanting to pee.

Then it stops. Restless as streetwalkers in the silence,
we pace up and down the fence. Blonde in black leather,
diminished, she wobbles on spikes out of haze.

Asks how come we're there — middle of nowhere.
We crowd around but she only laughs: *You think cops
will come. Ha! They never come.* And she staggers off.

Who knows what spurs on the guy, then, in the wrinkled
blue suit who suddenly leaps — a condemned man's last lunge —
up ten feet of wrought iron, swings one leg over the top,

balances endless seconds above spikes and razor wire,
before he flings the other over and jumps down
to our furious cheers. And who cares

by what right he rifles the cars for tools, and skilled
as a cat man, dismantles the lock — or by what right all of us,
lean our shoulders into the heavy gate, shove it back,

leap for our cars, and get the hell out of there.

DONOR

Every fifty-six days Walter went downtown,
stretched out on a hard mattress
and rolled up his sleeve
until he became the first person in Boston
ever to give twenty-five gallons of blood.
Nothing to it, he told THE GLOBE. *After
thirty years it's a snap and I'm better
off for it.* To WBZ he quipped:
I do it for the sandwiches, and shoved
the black cap left over from cabby days
back on hair gone wiry-gray,
his Irish face florid.

All Walter owns is closed behind French doors
in one square rooming house room:
on a walnut dresser a cracked St. Jude
and a fifth of vodka, seal ten years unbroken,
a symbol for something he might yet become.
No family to speak of except, in the veterans' home,
an older brother who failed suicide in the Metro.
His parents, having put the fear of God into him,
died young. He never married.
Nightly, he downs hot turkey sandwiches at Friendly's
hobnobbing with the local color. Most days,
he stays close to his room, folding socks,
riding a second-hand exercycle in front of the TV.
Before bed, he kneels in blue pajamas.

When in honor the Red Cross people raised
their glasses and the keynote speaker praised him
as *a philanthropist who's helped a thousand,*

he rose, looking out at that gray confusion —
not even one face, friend or kin — and joked:
*I've been called many things but no one
ever called me* that *before.* Imagine.
A thousand people, the slow red river
he's let over years.

DUBLIN BEGGAR

In the courtyard of St. Teresa of Avila's
just before mass
she sprawled on the stones,
her back against the building,
a thicket of black hair tangling across her face.
Her age was unknowable —
but nearly old — as I am nearly old,
skirts spread in billows around her like shadow.
I leaned down and touched her.
No, I leaned on the church wall and watched her.
No.

She made me sad and terrified.
You know how it is —
you don't know what helps and what doesn't.
You want to be good.
You want to walk away and not think about it.
I walked half a block beyond her, then turned
and went back.

As I dug through my change-purse for coins,
I tried to look into her ruined face;
she didn't look at me —
there was no sign that she saw me,
no sign she saw anything —
her black eyes focused on nothing
or on something far off beyond the high wall.

How can the spirit fall from the body —
who allows it and where does it go?
No one can carry it back after it's gone too far.
Beyond us, three tolls of the church bell,

and the twopence, the twenty pence
I tossed into the black hat
turned upside-down on the walk
made no sound when they fell.

VATHANA TELLS OF HER HUNGER*

You ask me how my father died, and my relatives.
Starving, I tell you, *all of them starving.*
After the Khmer Rouge came, after my family
had been driven out with the others from Phnom Penh,
in my village there was never enough, only the thin
bowl of rice, a bit of fish, and sometimes not that.
The weak fell quickly, were struck
in the back of their heads, left to die in ditches,
or carried off into a night of snakes and tigers.

Such evil memories: men and women hanging
from tree limbs, mangoes stuffed
into black mouth-holes, bodies on the ground,
their heads gaping beside them —
But it was always the hunger that hurt most,
my belly blown out like a pregnant woman, my hands
reaching for each stray bit of fruit.
Eat, eat, I'd say to my sister, to my uncle
as they turned and tossed in the sweat of malaria.
Eat, I'd say to my father, back from the fields,
his face swollen, his bowels running out of him.

---

*On April 17, 1975, the Khmer Rouge rebels marched into Phnom Penh and overthrew the Lon Nol government. They set up a collectively organized economy and engineered a program to "purify" the Khmer race. Buddhism, the state religion, was forbidden; the monks were massacred and the temples destroyed. The extermination of all educated classes was ordered, and, over four years, one third of the population (an estimated 1.7 million people) were murdered or died of hunger, disease or torture.

"The Angkar" was the people's organization of the Khmer Rouge; "bonzes" were monks; the "Yotear" were Khmer Rouge officials.

Before the Angkar (which sees everything
with the thousand eyes of the pineapple) forbade us
our Buddha, our pagodas and bonzes, I'd learned well
the Noble Truths: *All life is sorrow. Do not desire.*
Still I desired my life; I cherished
the silvery fish of the ponds, young green shoots
of the fields, the rice-wafer of moon above them.

If only there was not the hunger, and the hunger
turning to fear, the fear to anger in my stomach.
How I hated them, the Yotear, the Angkar,
all the men in black. I hated how they made me scythe
the wide swaths of rice, how they starved or murdered,
one by one, my father, my uncle, the villagers
who disappeared in the loud night.

I feigned illness one noon and walked back
to the work camp, packed a few provisions
in a rush basket, and pretended to return
to the paddies, strolling out slowly beneath the eyes

of the guards. Once beyond them, I ran. Ran past rice silos,
fuel depots, into the forest where spirits hovered
among the branches of the jacarandas, where snakes
coiled in every crevice.

I slept days, traveled, mostly in darkness,
across four provinces, wading calf-high in mud, bathing
in ponds, pulling off leeches.
And the hunger rose and fell in me, and the anger
was a steady fire.
I went on running and hiding all winter.

Here in America I've borne a son, whose lashes
are long and dark. His name is Phan; he is two

and his eyes are so clear that I think
he has lived many lives.
I scrub for swan-white women in big houses
west of the city. But I am not safe from the hunger,
the anger that day and night roars like an underground fire.
It rises up like a dragon — and undoes me.

I trust no one, will take nothing from anyone.
Is there no stopping this column of flame?
It threatens to swallow me whole like a mouse.
I fear for the son whom I love
beyond this life — beyond all life.
Day after day he refuses to eat.
Blood roars through my temples. I raise my hand at him.
I dig my fingernails into his arm and spoon the rice
as hard as I can against his locked lips.

THE CAMEO CARVERS OF TORRE DEL GRECO

They chip ash-white beauty
into shell as orange as if the lava
that flowed seven times over this village
to reach the sea had hardened
beneath cobalt waters and been flung back.

As if after the peasants scattered
to neighboring hilltops,
after churches turned to pyres
and the goat with the burning eyes ran off,
when vineyards smoldered to silence,

the sons of those exiles
picked themselves up,
shaking their heads, and went down
to the Bay of Naples, gathering
shells, gathering mountains of shells

bringing them back
to what was no longer there,
and on that pumice and volcanic rock
built (seven times) again,
out of nothing,

villas and terraces,
piazzas and vineyards,
not out of faith
or foolishness —
but some need to keep

the place where they belonged,
and in rough workshops
over long gray benches
taught themselves to chisel something
to endure,

passing this legacy from son to son
as if these amulets,
the color of burnt Italian earth,
the oval of sadness,
could stay Vesuvius.

ARGUING LIFE FOR LIFE

> *...arguing life for life even at your life's cost...*
> — *Muriel Rukeyser* *

Today in my office someone wanted to die
and I said *No*.

I leaned from the soft back of my chair
toward him as he bent forward, his back rounded
over his lap, his face in his huge hands.

I was long past menopause, family gone.
He didn't know this.

And I said *No, because you can't do this
to your children,* and *No, because
you won't always feel this way.*
I told him how time is aloe to the burn.

He said he had a loaded rifle beneath his bed.
He said he could turn his wheel toward the roadside gully.

I said *No* to this man before me,
and I could feel an energy rise from somewhere
deep in my body and cast out beyond me,
toward him — a hot energy — a river, a rope.
It wanted to pull him up.

He closed against it. He shut up like a cave door
overgrown with tangled thorns.
He went somewhere else —
narrow passage, so dark and steep

*from "Double Dialogue: Homage to Robert Frost"

I couldn't climb down.

I leaned back, let my hands fall;
both of us were tired of pain
and loss tallied week after week.

He didn't know how sometimes I stand
at my bedroom window looking out
where the white steeple lifts over the town,
wondering what is left to tether me to the earth.

We sat a long time bound in silence then.
It was all I knew how to do for us.

ABOUT THE AUTHOR

PATRICIA FARGNOLI holds a Bachelor of Arts from Trinity College in Hartford and a Master of Social Work from the University of Connecticut. Pat, who lives in Walpole, New Hampshire, is retired from her career as a clinical social worker and psychotherapist and currently teaches poetry at the Keene Institute of Music and Related Arts and in private tutorials. In the spring of 1998, she was awarded a fellowship at the MacDowell Colony, and she has been in residence several times at the Dorset Writer's Colony in Dorset, Vermont. She was on the resident faculty of The Frost Place Poetry Festival and is an Associate Editor of *The Worcester Review*. She has published widely in such literary journals as *Poetry, Ploughshares, Prairie Schooner, Poetry Northwest, The Laurel Review* and *The Indiana Review*. She was the recipient of the 1997 Robert Frost Literary Award, and the 1999 May Swenson Poetry Award for her book, *Necessary Light*. The book was also a semi-finalist for The 2001 Glascow Awards.

She has three adult children and two grandchildren.

WALKING TO WINDWARD

BOOKS IN THE SERIES *Walking to Windward* were set in Minion 11/14, with Minion display. Minion is a fully developed neohumanist text family designed by Robert Slimbach, San Francisco, and issued by Adobe in 1989.

The books were designed and composed by Sidney Hall, Jr. in Brookline, New Hampshire. 1000 copies were printed on acid-free paper.

OTHER POETRY BOOKS FROM OYSTER RIVER PRESS:

Along the Roads of the Universe ~ Por los caminos del universo. Poems & illustrations by Amor Halperin. Translated by Ida Halperin. Bilingual, 1997.

Crow Milk. Rick Agran, 1997.

Edged in Light. Jane Jordan, 1993.

Halcyon Time. Poems by Hugh Hennedy. Illustrated by Charles Chu, 1993.

Intense Experience: Social Psychology through Poetry. Fred Samuels, Ed. 31 poems, index of concepts, and an essay on the Eight Ages of Man by Erik Erikson, 1990.

Peace in Exile. David Oates, 1992.

Shadows and Sun ~ Ombres et Soleil. Writings of 1913-1952. by Paul Eluard. Illustrations from Picasso, Magritte, Chagall. Translated by Cicely Buckley, 1995.

Thoughts for the Free Life: LAO TSU to the present. C. Buckley, Editor, Illustrator. Lao Tsu, Sophocles, Cervantes, Neruda, Shakespeare, Native Americans, Thoreau, *et al.,* from 5 continents, 25 centuries. 3rd ed., 1997.

Under the Legislature of Stars: 62 New Hampshire Poets. R. Agran, H. Crill, M. DeCarteret, Editors, 1999.

What We Will Give Each Other. Sidney Hall, Jr. (Hobblebush Books) 1993.